Classic Recipes of
CAMBODIA

Classic Recipes of
CAMBODIA

TRADITIONAL FOOD AND COOKING
IN 30 AUTHENTIC DISHES

GHILLIE BAŞAN

LORENZ BOOKS

This edition is published by Lorenz Books,
an imprint of Anness Publishing Ltd,
108 Great Russell Street,
London WC1B 3NA;
info@anness.com

www.lorenzbooks.com;
www.annesspublishing.com;
twitter: @Anness_Books

If you like the images in this book
and would like to investigate using
them for publishing, promotions or
advertising, please visit our website
www.practicalpictures.com
for more information.

A CIP catalogue record for this book
is available from the British Library.

Publisher: Joanna Lorenz
Senior Editor: Felicity Forster
Photographer: Martin Brigdale
Home Economists: Lucy McKelvie
    and Bridget Sargeson
Designer: Nigel Partridge
Production Controller: Ben Worley

PUBLISHER'S NOTE

Although the advice and information
in this book are believed to be accurate
and true at the time of going to press,
neither the authors nor the publisher can
accept any legal responsibility or liability
for any errors or omissions that may
have been made nor for any inaccuracies
nor for any loss, harm or injury that
comes about from following instructions
or advice in this book.

PUBLISHER'S ACKNOWLEDGEMENTS

The publisher would like to thank the
following for the use of their images.
iStock: 6–7, 8t, 9, 10t, 10b, 11.

COOK'S NOTES

Bracketed terms are intended
for American readers.

For all recipes, quantities are
given in both metric and imperial
measures and, where appropriate,
in standard cups and spoons.
Follow one set of measures,
but not a mixture, because they
are not interchangeable.

Standard spoon and cup
measures are level. 1 tsp = 5ml,
1 tbsp = 15ml, 1 cup = 250ml/8fl oz.

Australian standard tablespoons
are 20ml. Australian readers should
use 3 tsp in place of 1 tbsp for
measuring small quantities.

American pints are 16fl oz/2 cups.
American readers should use
20fl oz/2.5 cups in place of 1 pint
when measuring liquids.

Electric oven temperatures in
this book are for conventional
ovens. When using a fan oven, the
temperature will probably need to be
reduced by about 10–20°C/20–40°F.
Since ovens vary, you should check
with your manufacturer's instruction
book for guidance.

The nutritional analysis given
for each recipe is calculated per
portion (i.e. serving or item), unless
otherwise stated. If the recipe gives
a range, such as Serves 4–6, then
the nutritional analysis will be for the
smaller portion size, i.e. 6 servings.
The analysis does not include
optional ingredients, such as salt
added to taste.

Medium (US large) eggs are used
unless otherwise stated.

Front cover shows Stir-fried Frog's
Legs – for recipe, see page 45.

Contents

Introduction

Cambodia is a captivating country with a lively, international atmosphere; it features natural wonders, awe-inspiring temples and a rich and fascinating culture. Although rice and fish are the staple foods, Cambodia's culinary traditions have been influenced by India, Thailand, China, Vietnam and France. As a result, there are many dishes that resemble these cuisines, especially that of Vietnam, with a strong emphasis on coconut milk, and spices and herbs – particularly garlic, ginger, lemon grass, chillies and coriander (cilantro). Cambodia also enjoys the French colonial legacy of fresh baguettes, ice cream and coffee. Armed with the correct equipment, the cooking is fairly easy – most of the work is actually in the preparation.

Left: Temple of Angkor Wat, Cambodia – the largest religious monument in the world.

Cambodian Cuisine

The cuisine of Cambodia is experiencing a revival. The capital, Phnom Penh, has emerged from economic ruin and military occupation to become a charismatic place to visit, with a vibrant and exuberant international ambience. There are Western bars and restaurants adjacent to Cambodian restaurants selling traditional Khmer dishes.

On the whole, Cambodian cuisine has served the needs of a peasant culture, partly due to the decades of severe destruction of the land and the people at hands of brutal regimes. But it should not be forgotten that the once mighty Khmer empire spread over large sections of Thailand, Laos and Vietnam as well as Cambodia, and would have played a big role in influencing the court cuisine at Hue, a city in central Vietnam, so Cambodian dishes would also have influenced Vietnamese ones.

Markets

The markets of Cambodia are lively, colourful and atmospheric. They display the country's fish, livestock and agricultural produce, while the aroma of freshly cooked snacks wafts from the many makeshift stalls and noodle shops.

Cambodian meals

Most Cambodian dishes are cooked in a wok, known locally as a *chnang khteak*. For breakfast most Cambodians eat rice porridge, *bobor*, often with the addition of a little fish or

Above: Net fishing for freshwater fish and shellfish is a daily task on the Mekong River.

pork. A traditional Cambodian meal almost always includes a soup, *samla*, which is eaten at the same time as the other courses. While rice is the country's staple, fish is the most important source of protein. Most of the fish eaten in Cambodia is freshwater, caught in the Tonlé Sap Lake or Mekong River. Traditionally, fish is eaten wrapped in herbs and lettuce leaves and dipped in the national fish sauce, *tuk trey*, which is similar to the Vietnamese *nuoc mam*.

Right: A sumptuous array of fruits in a market in Phnom Penh.

Below: Tuk trey, *a type of fish sauce, is a principal ingredient in many Cambodian dishes.*

Food and Festivals

Cambodia is a very traditional society with an emphasis on strong family values and religion, however the culinary customs tend to be fairly relaxed. When eating at home, diners sit on floor mats with their feet to the side rather than cross-legged. Traditionally, they would have

Below: Sticky rice wrapped in banana leaves is enjoyed during many Cambodian celebrations.

followed the long-established custom of using their hands to eat, but nowadays forks and chopsticks as well as hands are commonly used.

Family celebrations
At weddings and festive banquets, there are a number of sweet snacks made in the home or sold in the markets, such as sticky rice balls stuffed with banana, sticky rice cakes

Above: Festivities relating to water are important traditions in Cambodia. The reversal of the current of the Tonlé Sap signals a three-day celebration.

in banana leaves, and pumpkin pudding in banana leaves, or *nom l'poh*.

Festivals and holidays
There are many religious festivals and national holidays, such as the Day for Remembering the Victory over the Genocidal Regime (7 January); the Chinese New Year, which usually falls around the same time as the Vietnamese *Tet*; the King's

birthday; the Royal Ploughing Ceremony, *Chat Preah Nengkal*, held in early May in Phnom Penh to bless the farmers with successful crops in the coming year; the Khmer New Year; Buddha's birth, enlightenment and death; *Bon Om Tuk*; and Independence Day, which is celebrated on 9 November.

Khmer New Year

Chaul Chnam, the Khmer New Year, lasts for three days in mid-April. Pilgrimages are made to the temples of Angkor, and offerings are made at the temples and wats. Homes are cleaned out, gifts of new clothes are exchanged and food is shared. Water plays a key role in the celebrations, as it symbolizes cleansing and renewal.

Bon Om Tuk

This is one of the most important festivals in Cambodia. Held in early November, it is a celebration of the reversal of the current of the Tonlé Sap. Just as the dry season begins, the

water that is backed up in the lake begins to empty into the Tonlé Sap (the channel that links the lake to the Mekong) and on into the Mekong – a cause for much celebration. Boat races are held on the Tonlé Sap and on the moat around Angkor Wat.

Buddha's Birth, Enlightenment and Death

Cambodia celebrates these three events during a single celebration – Buddha Day – which falls on the 15th day

Above: It is traditional to make offerings of food and aroma sticks for events such as Khmer New Year and Buddha Day.

of the sixth lunar month. The joyful festivities take place at pagodas and temples, which are decorated with lanterns, food and aroma sticks. In the evening, a variety of processions take place – one of the most impressive is the candlelit procession of Buddhist monks at the ruins of Angkor Wat.

Classic Ingredients

The culinary culture of Cambodia has been influenced by the cuisines of India, Thailand, China and France, so there are inevitably many similarities. Fish and rice are the staples, and there is a strong emphasis on coconut milk combined with herbs and spices.

Rice and noodles

There are three main types of rice in Cambodia: long grain, short grain and sticky 'glutinous' rice. Traditionally, rice is boiled or steamed, then may be stir-fried; sticky rice is steamed until it resembles porridge (see panel).

Below: The stalks, leaves and flowers of the flowering cabbage are all edible.

If the main dish doesn't contain rice, it might instead consist of noodles. These are eaten at all hours of the day, in a soup for breakfast, stir-fried for a quick and filling snack, or incorporated into a main dish.

Vegetables

Whether raw, stir-fried, braised, pickled or salted, vegetables are worked into every meal in some manner in Cambodia. Almost every dish includes a few vegetables but, in addition, there may be a vegetable side dish, salad, pickled vegetables, or leaves to wrap around the food.

The most commonly used vegetables are aubergines (eggplant), bamboo shoots, long beans – sometimes referred to as 'snake beans' – dried beans, gourds and squashes, fresh and dried mushrooms, cabbages and greens such as pak choi (bok choy), flowering cabbage, mustard greens, preserved cabbage, Chinese leaves and water spinach. The crunchy texture of tubers and aquatic

Making sticky rice
Sticky, or glutinous, rice is often enjoyed as a snack.

1 Put 350g/12oz/1¾ cups sticky rice into a bowl and fill with cold water. Leave to soak for at least 6 hours, then drain, rinse thoroughly and drain again.

2 Fill a wok or heavy pan one-third full with water. Place a bamboo steamer, with the lid on, over the wok or pan and bring to the boil. Uncover and place a damp piece of muslin (cheesecloth) over the rack. Tip the rice into the middle and spread it out.
3 Fold the muslin over the rice, cover and steam for 25 minutes, until the rice is tender but still firm. The quantity of rice grains doubles when cooked.

Above: Coconut is a versatile and valuable fruit in Cambodia. Ripe fruits are used for making coconut milk, while the soft, young flesh makes a tasty snack.

roots is also enjoyed in salads and stir-fries. These include cassava, tapioca flour, mooli (daikon), lotus flower or water lily, taro and water chestnuts.

Fruit

Traditionally, fruit is reserved for the end of a meal, to cleanse the palate and aid the digestion.

Coconut (*dua*) is the most commonly used fruit for both sweet and savoury dishes in Cambodia. Both ripe and immature coconuts are used. Coconut milk (*nuoc dua*)

is the main cooking liquid in curries and puddings. It is used to enrich sauces and soups; boiled with sugar to make sweets wrapped in rice paper; and poured over sticky rice for a moist snack.

The next most popular fruit is banana (*chuoi*). Many puddings and desserts call for bananas, fresh or fried. Banana leaves are used as both cooking vessels and wrappers for fish and meat. Banana blossom is usually eaten raw and served in salads. It is prepared by slicing it finely and soaking in water with a

*Below: The lovely deep purple bud from the heart of the banana flower (*bap chuoi*) is enjoyed as a vegetable.*

Above: Encased in a spiky, armour-like skin, durian is creamy, dense and pungent. The yellow flesh of this large fruit has a strong, cheesy odour.

squeeze of lemon or lime juice to prevent it from discolouring.

Other commonly used fruits include: lychees; pineapples; fragrant red arbutus and the flowery rambutan; mango and papaya; juicy, brown-skinned longans; star fruit (carambola); watermelon-sized jackfruit; guavas; passion fruit; citrus fruits such as pomelo; mangosteens; coconuts and custard apples; green dragon fruit; and the infamous spiky durian, which is considered the 'king of fruit'.

Tofu products

An inexpensive protein food, tofu or bean curd (*dau hu*) is often referred to as 'poor man's meat' in Cambodia. It is used as an alternative to meat or fish, and it lends itself to stir-frying, grilling or broiling, steaming, smoking or simmering. There are dried, preserved, fermented and silken varieties.

Seafood

From their extensive coastlines, Cambodians get plentiful supplies of fish, such as grouper, mackerel, shark, red

Below: The firm, white flesh of sea bass is ideal for use in stews and curries. It is especially well suited to steaming.

snapper, tuna and sea bass, as well as shellfish, including crabs, squid and prawns or shrimp. From their rivers and lakes, they get carp and catfish, eels, freshwater shrimp and crab, and water-dwelling snails.

Dried and fermented fish products play a big role in the flavouring of stocks, stews and stir-fries in Cambodia. Generally, small fish and shellfish are dried whole for their texture and flavour.

Meat

The principal meat in Cambodia is pork; many families in the countryside may own a pig. A light, versatile meat, pork lends itself to every cooking method. It can also be salt- and air-cured and made into sausages. Cuts of fresh pork are usually eaten as a main dish, often combined with chicken or shellfish.

Beef appears in Khmer dishes such as spicy soups, and in zesty raw-beef salads in which the paper-thin slices of meat are tossed in fish sauce and lime juice.

Above: Slices of raw beef can be marinaded in a fiery mixture of oil, tuk trey *and soy sauce.*

For many years, under the brutal Khmer Rouge regime, frogs, lizards and insects formed part of the daily diet for many Cambodians, and they are still very popular in Cambodian cuisine. Frog's legs are often cooked in traditional stir-fries.

Poultry and eggs

Chickens and ducks are bred all over Cambodia, even in the densely populated neighbourhoods around the major cities. Small birds, such as quail and squab, are also common, often spit-roasted and devoured as a snack.

Above: Quail are so small that you can munch the whole bird in a matter of minutes.

Eggs are collected and used daily, occasionally added whole to dishes to symbolize fertility, good luck or happiness.

Herbs, spices and flavourings

Along with the national fish sauces, distinctive combinations of herbs and spices are what give Cambodia's food its unmistakeable character. Among the available herbs and spices that make up the colourful culinary picture are numerous varieties of mint, dill, coriander (cilantro), basil, thyme, oregano, chives, lemon grass,

ginger, the liquorice-flavoured star anise, turmeric, fresh and dried chillies, galangal, garlic and Chinese five-spice powder.

Other flavouring ingredients that shape Cambodian cuisine include tamarind, lotus seeds, tiger lilies, sugar cane, pandanus leaves, dried lily buds and limes. Peanuts – roasted and crushed – are frequently scattered over dishes for texture and garnish. Spring onions (scallions) are often cut into strips and added raw to soups, spring rolls and stir-fries.

Below: In Cambodian cuisine, lotus seeds are dried and then boiled to be used in festive sweets and cakes.

Above: Nuoc mam is a pungent fish sauce that is used in many Cambodian dishes.

Store-cupboard ingredients

Flavoured oils and sauces are essential in the Cambodian kitchen. These include groundnut (peanut) oil, sesame oil, soy sauce, chilli sauce and *kroeung* (a herbal paste). Fish-based products include the following indispensable store-cupboard ingredients: *tuk trey*, Cambodia's fish sauce; *nuoc mam*, a fermented fish sauce with a pungent smell; *mam tom*, a fermented shrimp paste; and *tuk prahoc*, a pungent condiment made by fermenting whole fish or chunks of fish with ground rice and salt.

Tastes of Cambodia

The wonderful recipes in this book have been drawn from many different areas of Cambodia – from the central Tonlé Sap region to the mangrove and palm-studded sandy beaches of the southern coast. With a strong emphasis on fresh ingredients and with all elements of the meal typically prepared from scratch, the selection of typical dishes presented here includes snacks and soups, fish and shellfish, meat and poultry, vegetables, rice and noodles, and sweet snacks. Together, the recipes provide an exciting introduction to the food and cooking of this charismatic and inspirational country.

Left: Two essentials of Cambodian cuisine, tamarind dipping sauce is popular with steamed or grilled fish and shellfish, and Cambodian herbal paste (kroeung) is used to flavour marinades, soups and stir-fries.

Crunchy Summer Rolls
Nem To-hu Sap

1 Pour some lukewarm water into a shallow dish. Then soak the rice papers, 2–3 at a time, for about 5 minutes until they are pliable. Place the soaked papers on a clean dish towel and then cover with a second dish towel to keep them moist.

2 Work with one paper at a time. Place a lettuce leaf towards the edge nearest to you, leaving about 2.5cm/1in to fold over. Place a mixture of the vegetables on top, followed by some mint and coriander leaves.

3 Fold the edge nearest to you over the filling, tuck in the sides, and roll tightly to the edge on the far side. Place the filled roll on a plate and cover with clear film or plastic wrap, so it doesn't dry out.

4 Repeat with the remaining rice papers and vegetables. Serve with a dipping sauce of your choice. If you are making these summer rolls ahead of time, keep them in the refrigerator under a damp dish towel, so that they remain moist.

COOK'S TIPS

• In Cambodia, these crunchy filled rolls are accompanied by a dipping sauce called *tuk trey*, but they are delicious when accompanied with many kinds of dipping sauce.
• The rice papers in which these rolls are wrapped can be bought in Chinese and South-east Asian markets.

Serves 4

12 round rice papers
1 lettuce, leaves separated and
    ribs removed
2–3 carrots, cut into julienne strips
1 small cucumber, peeled, halved
    lengthways and seeded, and cut
    into julienne strips
3 spring onions (scallions), trimmed
    and cut into julienne strips
225g/8oz mung beansprouts
1 bunch fresh mint leaves
1 bunch coriander (cilantro) leaves
dipping sauce, to serve
    (see Cook's Tips)

These delightful rice paper rolls filled with crunchy raw summer vegetables and fresh herbs are light and refreshing, and are eaten either as a snack or an appetizer to a meal. They are enjoyed throughout Cambodia.

Curried Sweet Potato Balls

Serves 4

450g/1lb sweet potatoes or taro root, boiled or baked, and peeled
30ml/2 tbsp sugar
15ml/1 tbsp Indian curry powder
25g/1oz fresh root ginger, peeled and grated
150g/5oz/1¼ cups glutinous rice flour or plain (all-purpose) flour
salt
sesame seeds or poppy seeds
vegetable oil, for deep-frying
dipping sauce, to serve

1 In a bowl, mash the cooked sweet potatoes or taro root. Beat in the sugar, curry powder and ginger. Add the rice flour (sift it if you are using plain flour) and salt, and work the mixture into a stiff dough – add more flour if necessary.

2 Pull off lumps of the dough and mould them into small balls – you should be able to make roughly 24 balls. Roll the balls on a bed of sesame seeds or poppy seeds until they are completely coated.

3 Heat enough oil for deep-frying in a wok. Fry the sweet potato balls in batches, until golden. Drain on kitchen paper. Serve the balls with wooden skewers to make it easier to dip them into a dipping sauce of your choice.

These sweet potato balls from Cambodia are delicious dipped in a fiery sauce, such as tuk trey, *fried black chilli sauce or hot peanut dipping sauce. Incredibly simple to make, they are ideal for serving as a nibble with a drink.*

Fried Squid with Salt and Pepper

Serves 4

450g/1lb baby or medium squid
30ml/2 tbsp coarse salt
15ml/1 tbsp ground black pepper
50g/2oz/½ cup rice flour or
    cornflour (cornstarch)
vegetable oil, for deep-frying
2 limes, halved

1 Prepare the squid by pulling the head away from the body. Sever the tentacles from the rest and trim them. Reach inside the body sac and pull out the backbone, then clean the squid inside and out, removing any skin. Rinse well in cold water.

2 Using a sharp knife, slice the squid into rings and pat them dry with kitchen paper. Put them in a dish with the tentacles. Combine the salt and pepper with the rice flour or cornflour, add it to the squid and toss well, making sure it is evenly coated.

3 Heat the oil for deep-frying in a wok or heavy pan. Cook the squid in batches, until the rings turn crisp and golden. Drain on kitchen paper and serve with limes to squeeze over. This dish can also be served with noodles, or with chunks of baguette and fresh chillies.

Cooking squid couldn't be simpler. Salt and pepper are used for seasoning – and that's it. A traditional method for cooking all sorts of fish and shellfish, this is a Cambodian favourite. Ideal snack and finger food, the tender squid can be served on its own.

Dry-cooked Pork Strips

Serves 2–4

15ml/1 tbsp groundnut (peanut) oil
30ml/2 tbsp *tuk trey*
30ml/2 tbsp soy sauce
5ml/1 tsp sugar
225g/8oz pork fillet, cut into thin,
    bitesize strips
8 lettuce leaves
chilli oil, for drizzling
fresh coriander (cilantro) leaves
a handful of fresh mint leaves

This Cambodian dish is quick and light on a hot day. Pork, chicken, prawns and squid can all be cooked this way. With the lettuce and herbs, it's a very flavoursome snack, but you can serve it with a dipping sauce, if you like.

1 In a wok or heavy pan, heat the oil, *tuk trey* and soy sauce with the sugar. Add the pork and stir-fry over a medium heat, until all the liquid has evaporated. Cook the pork until it turns brown, almost caramelized, but not burnt.

2 Drop spoonfuls of the cooked pork into lettuce leaves, drizzle a little chilli oil over the top, add a few coriander and mint leaves, wrap them up and serve immediately.

VARIATION

You could try basil, flat leaf parsley, spring onions (scallions) or sliced red onion in these tasty parcels.

Serves 4

30ml/2 tbsp groundnut (peanut)
   or vegetable oil
3 shallots, finely sliced
2 garlic cloves, finely chopped
2 Thai chillies, seeded and
   finely sliced
25g/1oz galangal, shredded
8 large, ripe tomatoes, skinned,
   seeded and finely chopped
15ml/1 tbsp sugar
30ml/2 tbsp *tuk trey*
4 lime leaves
900ml/1½ pints/3¾ cups
   chicken stock
15ml/1 tbsp wine vinegar
4 eggs
sea salt and ground black pepper

For the garnish

chilli oil, for drizzling
1 small bunch fresh coriander
   (cilantro), finely chopped
1 small bunch fresh mint leaves,
   finely chopped

Spicy Tomato and Egg Drop Soup

1 Heat the oil in a wok or heavy pan. Stir in the shallots, garlic, chillies and galangal and cook until golden and fragrant. Add the tomatoes with the sugar, *tuk trey* and lime leaves. Stir until it resembles a sauce. Pour in the stock and bring to the boil. Reduce the heat and simmer for 30 minutes. Season.

2 Just before serving, bring a wide pan of water to the boil. Add the vinegar and half a teaspoon of salt. Break the eggs into individual cups or small bowls.

3 Stir the water rapidly to create a swirl and drop an egg into the centre of the swirl. Follow immediately with the others, or poach two at a time, and keep the water boiling to throw the whites up over the yolks. Turn off the heat, cover the pan and leave to poach until firm enough to lift. Poached eggs are traditional, but you could use lightly fried eggs instead.

4 Using a slotted spoon, lift the eggs out of the water and slip them into the hot soup. Drizzle a little chilli oil over the eggs, sprinkle with the coriander and mint, and serve.

VARIATION

The soup is very tasty without the eggs, and could be served as a spicy tomato soup on its own.

Popular among the Chinese communities in Cambodia, this spicy soup with eggs is probably adapted from the traditional Chinese egg drop soup. Served on its own with chunks of crusty bread, or accompanied by jasmine or ginger rice, it is perfect for a light supper.

Duck and Preserved Lime Soup
Samlaw Tiah

1 Place the duck in a large pan with enough water to cover. Season with salt and pepper and bring the water to the boil. Reduce the heat, cover the pot, and simmer for 1½ hours.

2 Add the preserved limes and ginger. Continue to simmer for another hour, skimming off the fat from time to time, until the liquid has reduced a little and the duck is so tender that it almost falls off the bone.

3 Meanwhile, heat some vegetable oil in a wok. Stir in the ginger and garlic strips and fry until gold and crispy. Drain well on kitchen paper and set aside for garnishing.

4 Remove the duck from the broth and shred the meat into individual bowls. Check the broth for seasoning, then ladle it over the duck in the bowls. Scatter the spring onions with the fried ginger and garlic over the top and serve.

COOK'S TIPS
• With the addition of noodles, this soup could be served as a complete meal in itself.
• Preserved limes have a distinct bitter flavour. Look out for them in Asian markets.

Serves 4–6
1 lean duck, approximately
    1.5kg/3lb 5oz
2 preserved limes
25g/1oz fresh root ginger,
    thinly sliced
sea salt and ground black pepper

For the garnish
vegetable oil, for frying
25g/1oz fresh root ginger, thinly
    sliced into strips
2 garlic cloves, thinly sliced
    into strips
2 spring onions (scallions),
    finely sliced

This rich Cambodian soup has its origins in the Chiu Chow region of southern China. The recipe can be made with chicken stock and leftover duck meat from a roasted duck, or by roasting a duck and then slicing off the breast and thigh meat for the soup.

Serves 4

350g/12oz freshwater fish fillets,
  such as trout, cut into
  bitesize chunks
6 banana leaves
vegetable oil, for brushing
sticky rice, noodles or salad,
  to serve

For the marinade

2 shallots
5cm/2in turmeric root, peeled
  and grated
2 spring onions (scallions),
  finely sliced
2 garlic cloves, crushed
1–2 green Thai chillies, seeded
  and finely chopped
15ml/1 tbsp *tuk trey*
2.5ml/½ tsp raw cane sugar
salt and ground black pepper

Jungle Fish Cooked in Banana Leaves

1 To make the marinade, grate the shallots into a bowl, then combine with the other marinade ingredients. Season with salt and pepper. Toss the chunks of fish in the marinade, then cover and chill for 6 hours, or overnight.

2 Prepare a barbecue. Place one of the banana leaves on a flat surface and brush it with oil. Place the marinated fish on the banana leaf, spreading it out evenly, then fold over the sides to form an envelope. Place this envelope, fold side down, on top of another leaf and fold that one in the same manner. Repeat with the remaining leaves until they are all used up.

3 Secure the last layer of banana leaf with a piece of bendy wire. Place the banana leaf packet on the barbecue. Cook for about 20 minutes, turning it over from time to time to make sure it is cooked on both sides – the outer leaves will burn. Carefully untie the wire (it will be hot) and unravel the packet. Check that the fish is cooked, and serve with sticky rice, noodles or salad.

VARIATION
This banana leaf-wrapped dish can be made with any of the catfish or carp family, or even talapia.

Steaming freshwater fish in banana leaves over hot charcoal is a traditional method of cooking in the jungle. Banana leaves are large and tough, and serve as basic cooking vessels and wrappers for all sorts of fish and meat. Here, the fish is cooked in six layers of leaves, allowing for the outer ones to burn.

Fish in Coconut Custard Amok Trey

Serves 4

2 x 400ml/14oz cans coconut milk
3 eggs
80ml/3fl oz *kroeung*
15ml/1 tbsp *tuk trey*
10ml/2 tsp palm sugar or honey
1 kg/2¼lb fresh, skinned white
  fish fillets, cut into 8 pieces
1 small bunch chopped fresh
  coriander (cilantro), plus a few
  whole sprigs, to garnish
jasmine rice or crusty bread and
  salad, to serve

1 Half fill a wok or large pan with water. Set a bamboo or stainless steel steamer over it and put the lid on. Bring the water to the boil.

2 In a bowl, beat the coconut milk with the eggs, *kroeung*, *tuk trey* and sugar or honey, until it is well blended and the sugar has dissolved. Place the fish fillets in a heatproof dish that will fit in the steamer. Pour the coconut mixture over the fish and place the dish in the steamer.

3 Put the lid back on the steamer and reduce the heat so that the custard won't curdle. Steam over gently simmering water until the fish is cooked. Garnish with coriander and serve immediately with jasmine rice or crusty bread and salad.

VARIATION

If you don't have a big enough steamer, this dish can be cooked in the oven in a bain marie. Cook at 160°C/325°F/Gas 3 for about 50 minutes.

This rich and sumptuous Khmer classic crops up all over Cambodia. In Phnom Penh, there are restaurants that specialize in it. The fish is steamed in a custard, made with coconut milk and flavoured with the Cambodian herbal paste, kroeung.

Catfish Cooked in a Clay Pot Ca Kho To

Serves 4

30ml/2 tbsp sugar
15ml/1 tbsp sesame or vegetable oil
2 garlic cloves, crushed
45ml/3 tbsp *tuk trey*
350g/12oz catfish fillets, cut
    diagonally into 2 or 3 pieces
4 spring onions (scallions), cut
    into bitesize pieces
ground black pepper
chopped fresh coriander (cilantro),
    to garnish
fresh bread, to serve

Wonderfully easy and tasty, this Cambodian dish is a classic. Clay pots are regularly used for cooking, and they enhance both the look and taste of this traditional dish. Vary the recipe by adding chillies and other greens.

1 Place the sugar in a clay pot or heavy pan, and add 15ml/1 tbsp water to wet it. Heat the sugar until it begins to turn golden brown, then add the oil and crushed garlic.

2 Stir the *tuk trey* into the caramel mixture and add 120ml/4fl oz/½ cup boiling water, then toss in the catfish pieces, making sure they are well coated with the sauce. Cover the pot, reduce the heat and simmer for about 5 minutes.

3 Remove the lid, season with ground black pepper and gently stir in the spring onions. Simmer for a further 3–4 minutes to thicken the sauce, garnish with fresh coriander, and serve immediately straight from the pot with chunks of fresh bread.

Sea Bass Steamed in Coconut Milk with Ginger, Cashew Nuts and Basil

Serves 4

200ml/7fl oz coconut milk
10ml/2 tsp raw cane or muscovado (molasses) sugar
about 15ml/1 tbsp vegetable oil
2 garlic cloves, finely chopped
1 red Thai chilli, seeded and finely chopped
4cm/1½in fresh root ginger, peeled and grated
750g/1lb 10oz sea bass, gutted and skinned on one side
1 star anise, ground
1 bunch fresh basil, stalks removed
30ml/2 tbsp cashew nuts
sea salt and ground black pepper
rice and salad, to serve

1 Heat the coconut milk with the sugar in a small pan, stirring until the sugar dissolves, then remove from the heat. Heat the oil in a small frying pan and stir in the garlic, chilli and ginger. Cook until they begin to brown, then add the mixture to the coconut milk and mix well to combine.

2 Place the fish, skin side down, on a wide piece of foil and tuck up the sides to form a boat-shaped container. Using a sharp knife, cut several diagonal slashes into the flesh on the top and rub with the ground star anise. Season with salt and pepper and spoon the coconut milk over the top, making sure the fish is well coated.

3 Scatter half the basil leaves over the top of the fish and pull the foil packet almost closed. Lay the packet in a steamer. Cover the steamer, bring the water to the boil, reduce the heat and simmer for 20–25 minutes, or until just cooked. Alternatively, place the foil packet on a baking tray and cook in a preheated oven at 180°C/350°F/Gas 4.

4 Roast the cashew nuts in the frying pan, adding extra oil if necessary. Drain the nuts on kitchen paper, then grind them to crumbs. When the fish is cooked, lift it out of the foil and transfer it to a serving dish. Spoon the cooking juices over, sprinkle with the cashew nut crumbs and garnish with the remaining basil leaves. Serve with rice and a salad.

This is a delicious recipe for any whole white fish, such as sea bass or cod, or for large chunks of trout or salmon. You will need a steamer large enough to fit the whole fish or, if using fish chunks, you can use a smaller steamer and fit the fish around the base. The recipe also works well in the oven – place the fish, tucked in foil, on a tray and bake.

Stir-fried Long Beans with Prawns

Serves 4

450g/1lb fresh prawns (shrimp),
   shelled and deveined
45ml/3 tbsp vegetable oil
2 garlic cloves, finely chopped
25g/1oz galangal, finely shredded
1 onion, halved and finely sliced
450g/1lb long beans, trimmed and
   cut into 7.5cm/3in lengths
120ml/4fl oz/½ cup soy sauce

For the marinade

30ml/2 tbsp *tuk trey*
juice of 2 limes
10ml/2 tsp sugar
2 garlic cloves, crushed
1 lemon grass stalk, trimmed
   and finely sliced

1 To make the marinade, beat the *tuk trey* and the lime juice in a bowl with the sugar, until it has dissolved. Then stir in the garlic and lemon grass and mix together.

2 Toss in the prawns, cover the bowl, and chill for 1–2 hours.

3 Heat 30ml/2 tbsp of the oil in a wok. Stir in the chopped garlic and galangal. As they begin to colour, toss in the marinated prawns.

4 Stir-fry for a minute or until the prawns turn pink. Lift the prawns out, reserving as much of the oil, garlic and galangal as you can.

5 Add the remaining oil to the wok. Add the onion and stir-fry until slightly caramelized. Stir in the beans, then pour in the soy sauce. Cook for a further 2–3 minutes, until the beans are tender. Add the prawns and stir-fry for a minute until heated through. Serve immediately.

Long beans are a popular ingredient in Cambodia, and like many other vegetables they are often stir-fried with garlic. This recipe is livened up with prawns as well as other flavourings, and works well on its own with rice, or as a side dish.

Banana Blossom Salad with Prawns

1 Cut the banana blossom hearts into quarters lengthways and then slice them very finely crosswise. To prevent them discolouring, tip the pieces into a bowl of cold water mixed with the lemon juice and leave to soak for about 30 minutes.

2 To make the dressing, beat the lime juice, vinegar and *tuk trey* with the sugar in a small bowl, until it has dissolved. Stir in the chillies and garlic and set aside.

3 Drain the sliced banana blossom and put it in a bowl. Add the prawns and pour over the dressing. Toss well and garnish with the roasted peanuts, basil leaves and lime slices.

COOK'S TIP
Banana blossom doesn't actually taste of banana. Instead, it is mildly tannic, similar to an unripe persimmon – a taste and texture that complements chillies, lime and the local fish sauce.

VARIATION
If you cannot find any banana blossom hearts in Asian supermarkets, you can try this recipe with raw, or lightly steamed or roasted, fresh artichoke hearts.

Serves 4
2 banana blossom hearts
juice of 1 lemon
225g/8oz prawns (shrimp), cooked and shelled
30ml/2 tbsp roasted peanuts, finely chopped, fresh basil leaves and lime slices, to garnish

For the dressing
juice of 1 lime
30ml/2 tbsp white rice vinegar
60ml/4 tbsp *tuk trey*
45ml/3 tbsp palm sugar
3 red Thai chillies, seeded and finely sliced
2 garlic cloves, peeled and finely chopped

Banana blossom is very popular in Cambodia. The purplish-pink sheaths are used for presentation, the petals as a garnish, and the pointed, creamy yellow heart is tossed in salads, where it is combined with prawns, as here, or leftover grilled chicken, pork or tofu.

Stir-fried Beef with Sesame Sauce

Serves 4

450g/1lb beef sirloin or fillet,
  cut into thin strips
15ml/1 tbsp groundnut (peanut)
  or sesame oil
2 garlic cloves, finely chopped
2 red Thai chillies, seeded and
  finely chopped
7.5ml/1½ tsp sugar
30ml/2 tbsp sesame paste
30–45ml/2–3 tbsp beef stock
  or water
sea salt and ground black pepper
red chilli strips, to garnish
1 lemon, cut into quarters, to serve

For the marinade

15ml/1 tbsp groundnut (peanut) oil
30ml/2 tbsp *tuk trey*
30ml/2 tbsp soy sauce

*This dish is a real staple,
and variations can be found
all over Cambodia. Similar
to stir-fried beef with saté
(spicy peanut sauce), the
recipe has a deliciously
rich and nutty flavour.*

1 In a bowl, mix together the ingredients for the marinade. Toss in the beef, making sure it is well coated. Leave to marinate for 30 minutes.

2 Heat the groundnut or sesame oil in a wok or heavy pan. Stir in the garlic and chillies and cook until golden and fragrant. Stir in the sugar. Add the beef, tossing it around the wok to sear it.

3 Stir in the sesame paste and enough stock or water to thin it down. Cook for 1–2 minutes, making sure the beef is coated with the sauce.

4 Season with salt and pepper, garnish with chilli strips and and serve with lemon wedges.

VARIATION
Chicken breast fillet or pork fillet can be used instead of beef.

Raw Beef Salad with Peanuts
Pleah Saiko

1 In a bowl, mix 30ml/2 tbsp *tuk prahoc* with the juice of two limes, and 30ml/2 tbsp of the sugar, beating until the sugar has dissolved. Add the lemon grass, shallots and garlic and combine well. Toss in the slices of beef, cover and place in the refrigerator for 1–2 hours.

2 Meanwhile, in a small bowl, beat the remaining *tuk prahoc* with the juice of the third lime. Stir in the remaining sugar, until it dissolves, and put aside.

3 Put the beef slices, drained of any remaining liquid, in a clean bowl. Add the chilli, peanuts and coriander. Toss with the dressing, garnish with coriander leaves and serve immediately.

Serves 4

45ml/3 tbsp *tuk prahoc*
juice of 3 limes
45ml/3 tbsp palm sugar
2 lemon grass stalks, trimmed and
　finely sliced
2 shallots, peeled and finely sliced
2 garlic cloves, finely chopped
450g/1lb beef fillet, very finely sliced
1 red chilli, seeded and finely sliced
50g/2oz roasted, unsalted peanuts,
　finely chopped or crushed
1 small bunch fresh coriander
　(cilantro), finely chopped, plus
　extra leaves, to garnish

There are many recipes for beef salads throughout South-east Asia, such as the Vietnamese goi bo, *but this Cambodian recipe is quite distinctive because it uses the flavoursome fish extract* tuk prahoc *together with roasted peanuts.*

Wheat Noodles with Stir-fried Pork

Serves 4

225g/8oz pork loin, cut into
  thin strips
225g/8oz dried wheat noodles,
  soaked in lukewarm water
  for 20 minutes
15ml/1 tbsp groundnut (peanut) oil
2 garlic cloves, finely chopped
2–3 spring onions (scallions),
  trimmed and cut into
  bitesize pieces
45ml/3 tbsp *kroeung*
15ml/1 tbsp *tuk trey*
30ml/2 tbsp unsalted roasted
  peanuts, finely chopped
chilli oil, for drizzling

For the marinade

30ml/2 tbsp *tuk trey*
30ml/2 tbsp soy sauce
15ml/1 tbsp peanut oil
10ml/2 tsp sugar

*Sold dried in straight
bundles like sticks, wheat
noodles are versatile and
robust. This simple recipe
comes from a noodle
stall in Phnom Penh.*

1 In a bowl, combine the ingredients for the marinade, stirring constantly until the all the sugar dissolves. Toss in the strips of pork, making sure they are well coated in the marinade. Then put aside for 30 minutes.

2 Drain the wheat noodles. Bring a large pan of water to the boil. Drop in the noodles, untangling them with chopsticks if necessary. Cook for 4–5 minutes, until tender. Allow the noodles to drain thoroughly, then divide them among individual serving bowls. Keep the noodles warm until the dish is ready to serve.

3 Meanwhile, heat a wok. Add the oil and stir-fry the garlic and spring onions, until fragrant. Add the pork, tossing it around the wok for 2 minutes.

4 Stir in the *kroeung* and *tuk trey* for 2 minutes – add a splash of water if the wok gets too dry – and tip the pork on top of the noodles. Sprinkle the peanuts over the top and drizzle with chilli oil to serve.

Chicken with Young Ginger
Cha Kngey Sach Mon

Serves 4

30ml/2 tbsp groundnut (peanut) oil
3 garlic cloves, finely sliced in strips
50g/2oz fresh young root ginger,
    finely sliced in strips
2 Thai chillies, seeded and finely
    sliced in strips
4 chicken breast fillets or 4 boned
    chicken legs, skinned and cut
    into bitesize chunks
30ml/2 tbsp *tuk prahoc*
10ml/2 tsp sugar
1 small bunch coriander (cilantro)
    stalks removed, roughly chopped
ground black pepper
jasmine rice and crunchy salad
    or baguette, to serve

*Ginger plays a big role
in Cambodian cooking,
particularly in the stir-fried
dishes. Whenever possible,
the juicier and more
pungent young ginger
is used. This is a simple
and tasty way to cook
chicken, pork or beef.*

1 Heat a wok or heavy pan and add the oil. Add the garlic, ginger and chillies, and stir-fry until fragrant and golden. Add the chicken and toss it around the wok for 1–2 minutes.

2 Stir in the *tuk prahoc* and sugar, and stir-fry for a further 4–5 minutes until cooked. Season with pepper and add some of the fresh coriander.

3 Transfer the chicken to a serving dish and garnish with the remaining coriander. Serve hot with jasmine rice and a crunchy salad with fresh herbs, or with chunks of freshly baked baguette.

Stir-fried Frog's Legs Ung Kep Char Kroeung

Serves 3–4

15ml/1 tbsp groundnut (peanut) oil
2 garlic cloves, finely chopped
2 Thai chillies, seeded and
    finely chopped
30ml/2 tbsp *kroeung*
15ml/1 tbsp *tuk prahoc*
15ml/1 tbsp palm sugar
4 fresh kaffir lime leaves
6 pairs of frog's legs, separated
    into 12 single legs, rinsed and
    dabbed dry
chilli oil, for drizzling

1 Heat the oil in a wok or heavy pan. Stir in the garlic and chillies, until they become fragrant. Add the *kroeung*, *tuk prahoc* and sugar and stir-fry until it begins to colour. Add the lime leaves and frog's legs, tossing them around the wok to make sure they are coated in the sauce. Arrange the legs against the base and sides of the wok to fry on both sides, until brown and crisp.

2 Transfer the frog's legs to a warmed serving dish and drizzle with chilli oil. Serve with garlic and ginger rice and a salad.

COOK'S TIP
Frog's legs, often sold in pairs, can be bought fresh and frozen in Asian markets. They are prized for stir-fries, where they are typically cooked with garlic and herbs.

Frog's legs are popular in Cambodia. Sold live in the markets, plump frogs are beheaded, skinned and cleaned for keen cooks, as the whole frog is edible. This is one of the most delicious ways of cooking frog's legs – with richly fragrant kroeung.

Pickled Vegetables

Serves 4–6

300ml/½ pint/1¼ cups white
    rice vinegar
90g/3½oz/½ cup sugar
450g/1lb carrots, cut into 5cm/2in
    matchsticks
450g/1lb mooli (daikon), halved
    lengthways and cut into
    thin crescents
600g/1lb 6oz cucumber, partially
    peeled in strips and cut into
    5cm/2in matchsticks
15ml/1 tbsp salt

1 In a large bowl, whisk the vinegar with the sugar, until it dissolves.

2 Add the carrots and mooli to the vinegar mixture and toss well to coat. Cover the vegetables and place in the refrigerator for 24 hours, turning them occasionally.

3 Put the cucumber on a plate and sprinkle with the salt. Leave for 30 minutes, then rinse under cold water and drain well. Add to the carrot and mooli and toss well in the pickling liquid. Cover and chill in the refrigerator as before.

4 Lift the vegetables out of the pickling liquid to serve, or spoon them into a jar and store in the refrigerator.

COOK'S TIP
White rice vinegar is acidic and keeps bacteria at bay, so these pickled vegetables can be kept in the refrigerator for up to three weeks.

Everyday Cambodian pickles generally consist of carrot, mooli and cucumber, which are orange, white and green in colour. They are great for nibbling on, as part of a table salad, or as an accompaniment to grilled meats and shellfish.

Soya Beansprout Salad

Serves 4

450g/1lb fresh soya beansprouts
2 spring onions (scallions),
    finely sliced
1 small bunch fresh coriander
    (cilantro), stalks removed

For the dressing

15ml/1 tbsp sesame oil
30ml/2 tbsp *tuk trey*
15ml/1 tbsp white rice vinegar
10ml/2 tsp palm sugar
1 red chilli, seeded and finely sliced
15g/½oz fresh young root ginger,
    finely shredded

*High in protein and fat, soya
beansprouts are particularly
favoured in Cambodia.
Unlike mung beansprouts,
they are slightly poisonous
when raw, and therefore
need to be parboiled before
using. Tossed in a salad,
they are often eaten with
noodles and rice.*

1 First make the dressing. In a bowl, beat the oil, *tuk trey* and rice vinegar with the sugar, until it dissolves. Stir in the chilli and ginger and leave to stand for 30 minutes to allow the flavours to develop.

2 Bring a pan of salted water to the boil. Drop in the beansprouts and blanch for a minute only. Drain and refresh under cold water until cool. Then drain again and put them into a clean dish towel. Shake out the excess water.

3 Put the beansprouts into a bowl with the spring onions. Pour over the dressing and toss well. Garnish with coriander leaves and serve.

Green Mango Salad Neorm Svye Kchey

Serves 4

450g/1lb green mangoes
grated rind and juice of 2 limes
30ml/2 tbsp sugar
30ml/2 tbsp *tuk trey*
2 green Thai chillies, seeded
    and finely sliced
1 small bunch fresh coriander
    (cilantro), stalks removed,
    finely chopped
salt

1 Peel, halve and stone (pit) the green mangoes, and slice them into thin strips.

2 In a bowl, mix together the lime rind and juice, sugar and *tuk trey*. Add the mango strips with the chillies and coriander.

3 Add salt to taste and leave to stand for 20 minutes to allow the flavours to mingle before serving.

COOK'S TIP

To remove the stone from a mango, hold the mango upright with the stem at the top. Turn the fruit so the widest side is nearest you. Cut all the way around to make two halves, then pull the halves away from the stone. The mango flesh can then be sliced into strips.

Although orange and yellow mangoes and papayas are devoured in vast quantities when ripe and juicy, they are also popular when green. Their tart flavour and crunchy texture make them ideal for salads and stews, or simply served with grilled prawns.

Rice Porridge with Fish Bobor

Serves 6

15ml/1 tbsp vegetable or groundnut
(peanut) oil
25g/1oz fresh root ginger, shredded
115g/4oz/generous 1 cup long grain
rice, rinsed and drained
1.2 litres/2 pints/5 cups chicken
stock or water
30–45ml/2–3 tbsp *tuk trey*
10ml/2 tsp sugar
450g/1lb fresh fish fillets, boned
(any fish will do)
sea salt and ground black pepper

For the garnish

15ml/1 tbsp vegetable or groundnut
(peanut) oil
2 garlic cloves, finely chopped
1 lemon grass stalk, trimmed
and finely sliced
25g/1oz fresh root ginger, shredded
a few coriander (cilantro) leaves

*A steaming bowl of thick
rice porridge is a nourishing
and satisfying breakfast. It
can be made plain, or with
the addition of chicken,
pork, fish or prawns.*

1 In a heavy pan, heat the oil and stir in the ginger and rice for 1 minute. Pour in the stock and bring it to the boil. Reduce the heat and simmer, partially covered, for 20 minutes, until the rice is tender and the soup is thick. Stir the *tuk trey* and sugar into the soupy porridge. Season and keep the porridge hot.

2 Meanwhile, fill a wok a third of the way with water. Fit a covered bamboo steamer on top and bring the water to the boil so that the steam rises. Season the fish fillets, place them on a plate and put them inside the steamer. Cover and steam until the fish is cooked.

3 For the garnish, heat the oil in small wok or heavy pan. Add the chopped garlic, sliced lemon grass and shredded ginger and stir-fry until golden and fragrant.

4 Ladle the rice porridge into bowls. Tear off pieces of steamed fish fillet to place on top. Sprinkle with the stir-fried garlic, lemon grass and ginger, and garnish with a few coriander leaves.

Fresh Rice Noodles

Serves 4

225g/8oz/2 cups rice flour
600ml/1 pint/2½ cups water
a pinch of salt
15ml/1 tbsp vegetable oil, plus extra
    for brushing
slivers of red chilli and fresh root
    ginger, and coriander (cilantro)
    leaves, to garnish (optional)

*Freshly made noodle sheets
can be served as a snack,
drenched in sugar or honey,
or dipped into a savoury
sauce of your choice.
Otherwise, cut them into
wide strips and gently
stir-fry with garlic, ginger,
chillies and tuk trey dipping
sauce or soy sauce.*

1 Place the rice flour in a bowl and stir in some of the water to form a paste. Pour in the rest of the water, beating it to make a lump-free batter. Add the salt and oil and leave to stand for 15 minutes.

2 Meanwhile, fill a wide pan with water. Cut a piece of smooth cotton cloth a little larger than the diameter of the pan. Stretch it over the top of the pan, pulling the edges tautly down over the sides, then wind a piece of string around the edge, to secure. Using a sharp knife, make three small slits, about 2.5cm/1in from the edge of the cloth, at regular intervals. These will allow steam to escape during cooking.

3 Bring the water to the boil. Stir the batter and ladle 30–45ml/2–3 tbsp on to the cloth, swirling it to form a 13–15cm/5–6in wide circle. Cover with a domed lid, such as a wok lid, and steam for 1 minute, or until the noodle sheet is translucent.

4 Carefully insert a spatula or knife under the noodle sheet and prise it off the cloth. (If it doesn't peel off easily, you may need to steam it a little longer.) Transfer the noodle sheet to a lightly oiled baking tray, brush gently with oil, and cook the remaining batter in the same way. Garnish with chilli, ginger and coriander, if you like.

COOK'S TIP

If the water runs low during the steaming process, you may need to top up with more water through one of the slits, then tighten the cloth.

Sticky Rice with Durian Sauce

1 Drain the sticky rice. Fill a wok a third of the way up with water. Fit a bamboo steamer into the wok and put the lid on. Bring the water to the boil, place a piece of dampened muslin (cheesecloth) over the bamboo rack and spoon the rice into it, leaving space all around for the steam to come through.

2 Carefully fold the muslin over the rice, cover the steamer, and steam for about 20 minutes, until the rice is translucent and tender but still has a bite to it. In a heavy pan, heat the coconut milk with a pinch of salt and the sugar, until it has dissolved.

3 Beat in the puréed durian. Pour a little less than half of the mixture into a small pan and set aside. Add the cooked rice to the remaining mixture and mix well. Put the lid on the pan and simmer for a further 15 minutes. Divide the sweetened rice among individual bowls. Heat the reserved sauce in the small pan and pour it over the rice.

Serves 4–6

115g/4oz/generous ½ cup sticky glutinous rice, rinsed, and soaked in plenty of water for at least 6 hours
550ml/18fl oz/2½ cups coconut milk
30ml/2 tbsp palm sugar
115g/4oz fresh durian flesh, puréed
salt

Throughout Cambodia, people often enjoy a snack of sweet sticky rice. Every culture has their own favourite version of this snack – some like it served with sweetened red beans, others with mango, but the Cambodians eat it with a dollop of durian sauce.

Cassava Sweet

Serves 6–8

butter, for greasing
350ml/12fl oz/1½ cups coconut milk
115g/4oz/generous ½ cup palm
    sugar
2.5ml/½ tsp ground aniseed
salt
675g/1½lb cassava root, peeled
    and coarsely grated

This type of sweet and sticky snack is usually served with a cup of light jasmine tea. More like an Indian helva *than a cake, this recipe can also be made using sweet potatoes or yams in place of the cassava.*

1 Preheat the oven to 190°C/375°F/Gas 5, and grease a ramekin or baking dish with butter. In a bowl, whisk the coconut milk with the palm sugar, ground aniseed and a pinch of salt, until the sugar has dissolved.

2 Beat the grated cassava root into the coconut mixture and pour into the greased ramekin or baking dish. Place it in the oven and bake for about 1 hour, or until it is golden on top. Leave the sweet to cool a little in the dish before serving warm or at room temperature.

COOK'S TIP

To prepare the cassava for grating, use a sharp knife to split the whole length of the root, and then carefully peel off the skin. Simply grate the peeled root using a coarse grater.

Pumpkin Pudding in Banana Leaves Nom L'Poh

Serves 6

1 small pumpkin, about 1.3kg/3lb,
    peeled, seeded and cubed
250ml/8fl oz/1 cup coconut milk
45ml/3 tbsp palm sugar
15ml/1 tbsp tapioca starch
12 banana leaves, cut into
    15cm/6in squares
salt

1 Bring a pan of salted water to the boil. Add the pumpkin flesh and cook for 15 minutes, or until tender. Drain and mash with a fork, or purée in a blender.

2 In a pan, heat the coconut milk with the sugar and a pinch of salt. Blend the tapioca starch with 15ml/1 tbsp water and 15ml/1 tbsp of the hot coconut milk. Add it to the coconut milk and beat well.

3 Beat the mashed pumpkin into the coconut milk or, if using a blender, add the coconut milk to the pumpkin and purée together.

4 Spoon equal amounts of the pumpkin purée into the centre of each banana leaf square. Fold in the sides and thread a cocktail stick or toothpick through the open ends to enclose the purée.

5 Fill the bottom third of a wok with water. Place a bamboo steamer on top. Place as many stuffed banana leaves as you can into the steamer, folded side up – you may have to cook them in batches. Cover the steamer and steam parcels for 15 minutes. Unwrap them and serve either hot or cold.

VARIATION

You can also try sweet potatoes, cassava or taro root in place of the pumpkin in this recipe.

This traditional pudding is native to Cambodia and it can be made with either small, sweet pumpkins or butternut squash. It is a very moreish dessert or snack which can be eaten hot, at room temperature, or cold.

Golden Threads Vawee

1 In a heavy pan, stir the water and sugar over a high heat, until the sugar dissolves. Bring to the boil, then reduce the heat and continue to stir for 5–10 minutes, until it begins to thicken. Add the rose water and continue to boil gently for 2–3 minutes. Pour the egg yolk into a piping or icing bag, or use a jug or pitcher with a narrow spout.

2 Carefully drip some of the egg yolk into the simmering syrup, moving backwards and forwards to form long threads, or in a circular motion to form round ones. Cook the threads for about 30 seconds, then, using a slotted spoon or chopsticks, lift them out of the syrup and on to a dish. Continue with the rest of the egg yolk, cooking in batches. Serve the threads as a snack, or to garnish sweet rice dishes and fruit salads.

Serves 2–4

450ml/¾ pint/scant 2 cups water
225g/8oz/generous 1 cup caster
　(superfine) sugar
30ml/2 tbsp rose water
12 egg yolks, lightly beaten
　together, and strained through
　a sieve or strainer

Frequently sold as a snack in the street markets of Cambodia, these delicate golden threads made from sugar, rose water and egg yolks are also used in restaurants as a decorative garnish for some of the custards and rice puddings.

Nutritional Notes

Sticky Rice: Energy 314Kcal/1314kJ; Protein 7g; Carbohydrate 66g, of which sugars 0g; Fat 1g, of which saturates 0g; Cholesterol 0mg; Calcium 14mg; Fibre 0g; Sodium 0mg.

Crunchy Summer Rolls: 106Kcal/445kJ; Protein 3.5g; Carbohydrate 21.2g, of which sugars 4.7g; Fat 0.7g, of which saturates 0.2g; Cholesterol 0mg; Calcium 44mg; Fibre 2.2g; Sodium 10mg.

Curried Sweet Potato Balls: Energy 354Kcal/1495kJ; Protein 5g; Carbohydrate 61g, of which sugars 14.8g; Fat 11.8g, of which saturates 1.5g; Cholesterol 0mg; Calcium 84mg; Fibre 3.9g; Sodium 50mg.

Fried Squid with Salt and Pepper: Energy 339Kcal/1405kJ; Protein 14g; Carbohydrate 5g, of which sugars 0g; Fat 29g, of which saturates 4g; Cholesterol 146mg; Calcium 70mg; Fibre 0g; Sodium 140mg.

Dry-cooked Pork Strips: Energy 96Kcal/401kJ; Protein 12.2g; Carbohydrate 0.4g, of which sugars 0.4g; Fat 5g, of which saturates 1.1g; Cholesterol 35mg; Calcium 7mg; Fibre 0.1g; Sodium 300mg.

Spicy Tomato and Egg Drop Soup: Energy 181Kcal/756kJ; Protein 8g; Carbohydrate 12.3g, of which sugars 11.5g; Fat 11.7g, of which saturates 2.4g; Cholesterol 190mg; Calcium 52mg; Fibre 2.3g; Sodium 280g.

Duck and Preserved Lime Soup: Energy 124Kcal/520kJ; Protein 19.8g; Carbohydrate 0.3g, of which sugars 0.3g; Fat 6.5g, of which saturates 1.3g; Cholesterol 110mg; Calcium 19mg; Fibre 0g; Sodium 100mg.

Jungle Fish Cooked in Banana Leaves: Energy 155Kcal/648kJ; Protein 18g; Carbohydrate 4g, of which sugars 2g; Fat 8g, of which saturates 1g; Cholesterol 59mg; Calcium 36mg; Fibre 0.7g; Sodium 200mg.

Fish in Coconut Custard: Energy 309Kcal/1304kJ; Protein 51.1g; Carbohydrate 12.4g, of which sugars 12.4g; Fat 6.5g, of which saturates 1.8g; Cholesterol 258mg; Calcium 103mg; Fibre 0g; Sodium 400mg.

Catfish Cooked in a Clay Pot: Energy 126Kcal/533kJ; Protein 16g; Carbohydrate 10g, of which sugars 8g; Fat 3g, of which saturates 0g; Cholesterol 40mg; Calcium 25mg; Fibre 0.2g; Sodium 600mg.

Sea Bass Steamed in Coconut Milk with Ginger, Cashew Nuts and Basil: Energy 235Kcal/983kJ; Protein 26g; Carbohydrate 8g, of which sugars 6g; Fat 11g, of which saturates 2g; Cholesterol 100mg; Calcium 217mg; Fibre 0.3g; Sodium 300mg.

Stir-fried Long Beans with Prawns: Energy 215Kcal/897kJ; Protein 23g; Carbohydrate 10g, of which sugars 8.2g; Fat 9g, of which saturates 1g; Cholesterol 219mg; Calcium 140mg; Fibre 2.7g; Sodium 235mg.

Banana Blossom Salad with Prawns: Energy 103Kcal/438kJ; Protein 11g; Carbohydrate 15g, of which sugars 13g; Fat 0.5g, of which saturates 0.1g; Cholesterol 110mg; Calcium 54mg; Fibre 0.7g; Sodium 109mg.

Stir-fried Beef with Sesame Sauce: Energy 269Kcal/1119kJ; Protein 26.2g; Carbohydrate 2/0g, of which sugars 2.0g; Fat 18g, of which saturates 5g; Cholesterol 65mg; Calcium 31mg; Fibre 0.3g; Sodium 73mg.

Raw Beef Salad with Peanuts: Energy 321Kcal/1343kJ; Protein 29g; Carbohydrate 15g, of which sugars 14g; Fat 16g, of which saturates 5g; Cholesterol 65mg; Calcium 48mg; Fibre 1.6g; Sodium 78mg.

Wheat Noodles with Stir-fried Pork: Energy 357Kcal/1494kJ; Protein 17g; Carbohydrate 51g, of which sugars 4.8g; Fat 9g, of which saturates 2g; Cholesterol 35mg; Calcium 21mg; Fibre 0.7g; Sodium 495mg.

Chicken with Young Ginger: Energy 222Kcal/935kJ; Protein 36.4g; Carbohydrate 3g, of which sugars 2.9g; Fat 7.3g, of which saturates 1.1g; Cholesterol 105mg; Calcium 32mg; Fibre 0.6g; Sodium 100mg.

Stir-fried Frog's Legs: Energy 113Kcal/475kJ; Protein 12.4g; Carbohydrate 8.5g, of which sugars 8.2g; Fat 3.4g, of which saturates 0.5g; Cholesterol 35mg; Calcium 22mg; Fibre 0.5g; Sodium 480mg.

Pickled Vegetables: Energy 104Kcal/438kJ; Protein 2g; Carbohydrate 24g, of which sugars 24g; Fat 0.5g, of which saturates 0.2g; Cholesterol 0mg; Calcium 59mg; Fibre 3.1g; Sodium 1013mg.

Aubergine Curry with Coconut Milk: Energy 72Kcal/305kJ; Protein 1.6g; Carbohydrate 11.2g, of which sugars 10.7g; Fat 3g, of which saturates 1g; Cholesterol 0mg; Calcium 46mg; Fibre 2.8g; Sodium 113mg.

Stir-fried Pineapple with Ginger: Energy 185Kcal/780kJ; Protein 3g; Carbohydrate 24.1g, of which sugars 23.6g; Fat 9g, of which saturates 1g; Cholesterol 0mg; Calcium 43mg; Fibre 2.9g; Sodium 271mg.

Glazed Pumpkin in Coconut Milk: Energy 114Kcal/477kJ; Protein 1.5g; Carbohydrate 14g, of which sugars 13.4g; Fat 6g, of which saturates 1g; Cholesterol 0mg; Calcium 68mg; Fibre 1.7g; Sodium 323mg.

Soya Beansprout Salad: Energy 76Kcal/317kJ; Protein 3.4g; Carbohydrate 8.6g, of which sugars 6.5g; Fat 3.3g, of which saturates 0.5g; Cholesterol 0mg; Calcium 27mg; Fibre 1.8g; Sodium 6mg.

Green Mango Salad: Energy 92Kcal/391kJ; Protein 1g; Carbohydrate 22g, of which sugars 15g; Fat 0g; Cholesterol 0mg; Calcium 32mg; Fibre 33g; Sodium 0.5g.

Rice Porridge with Fish: Energy 152Kcal/636kJ; Protein 15g; Carbohydrate 17g, of which sugars 1.7g; Fat 2g, of which saturates 0.3g; Cholesterol 35mg; Calcium 11mg; Fibre 0g; Sodium 45mg.

Fresh Rice Noodles: Energy 251Kcal/1046kJ; Protein 4g; Carbohydrate 45g, of which sugars 0g; Fat 5g, of which saturates 1g; Cholesterol 0mg; Calcium 24mg; Fibre 1.1g; Sodium 200mg.

Sticky Rice with Durian Sauce: Energy 111Kcal/470kJ; Protein 2g; Carbohydrate 25.4g, of which sugars 10g; Fat 0.4g, of which saturates 0.2g; Cholesterol 0mg; Calcium 39mg; Fibre 0.2g; Sodium 101mg.

Cassava Sweet: Energy 254Kcal/1086kJ; Protein 1g; Carbohydrate 64g, of which sugars 25g; Fat 1g, of which saturates 1g; Cholesterol 2mg; Calcium 39mg; Fibre 1.8g; Sodium 0.2g.

Pumpkin Pudding in Banana Leaves: Energy 60Kcal/257kJ; Protein 1g; Carbohydrate 13.6g, of which sugars 12.7g; Fat 0.5g, of which saturates 0.3g; Cholesterol 0mg; Calcium 64mg; Fibre 1.7g; Sodium 46mg.

Golden Threads: Energy 1619Kcal/6811kJ; Protein 36g; Carbohydrate 235g, of which sugars 235g; Fat 66g, of which saturates 19g; Cholesterol 2419mg; Calcium 400mg; Fibre 0g; Sodium 122mg.

Index